BUDDHA POEMS

© Text and cover image Nick Totton 2020

Published by Magpie Moon
4 Middleway
St Blazey
Par PL4 2JH
UK
ISBN 9798687527774

Nick Totton

Buddha Poems

*love from
Nick
xxxx*

Buddha on TV

They are making a TV film about the Buddha. He turns up on time, and does a single take; he is quietly pleased with his performance, despite a couple of minor rough edges. When he watches the finished film, however, the Buddha is uncomfortable: it seems a long time before he appears, and then he hardly recognises himself. Who is that presenter, anyway, and what is his angle? He hopes they are going to focus on issues, not personalities.

Travelling Buddha

The Buddha has difficulty travelling by train: being absent minded, he forgets where he has put his ticket. After several embarrassing mid-journey hunts under the eyes of the waiting inspector, the Buddha develops a strategy: he writes himself a note to remind him where he has put the ticket. Unfortunately, he then mislays the note. Eventually, the Buddha travels with a note in every pocket, each saying: 'Your ticket is in your wallet'. In his wallet, however, he finds only an identical note.

Buddha Is House Hunting

It's an old house, but sturdy. The Buddha might be interested, if the price is right. Are fixtures and fittings included? What about the carpets? The Buddha believes in value for money. The Buddha rings the door bell, fruitlessly, then goes round to the side entrance; the lights are on and there's a smell of cooking, but no one's home. Somewhere inside, a door starts to bang irregularly. The Buddha waits another minute or two, then turns and walks off quickly, shoulders hunched against the wind.

Buddha's Present

It's the Buddha's birthday, and he is excited – he has received a parcel in the post, marked 'Open Your Birthday, It's the Present'. It is a large cardboard box; when he opens it he finds colourful wrapping paper, which he quickly tears off, then a good deal of tissue paper, to avoid damage. Inside the tissue paper there is nothing. This is the best present ever, thinks the Buddha!

Covid Buddha

The Buddha has been told to self-isolate, but he is finding it difficult. *Can* the self be isolated? And if so, who is doing the isolating? He doesn't want to be awkward, but this strikes him as a fundamental question. However, the medics seem preoccupied and not very interested. Perhaps because he is running a temperature, he is unable to reach a firm conclusion.

Buddha the Translator

The Buddha is translating a book, a collection of his own talks. It's not a straightforward process: reading them now, the talks seem rather repetitive, probably because he was trying to make them easy to remember. Also, the concepts are quite difficult to translate. So should he leave the text as it is – it has after all been quite successful – or update it for the modern age? He tries boiling it down to the essential message, but the result seems too simple to be taken seriously.

Buddha Looks for a Job

The Buddha has decided the translation game is not for him, and he wants to try something else. He consults an employment agency, who ask him to fill in a form about his interests and qualifications. He answers to the best of his ability, but wonders whether he has really done himself justice – he has worn many hats over the years, as it were. The Buddha explains that he is not seeking anything permanent.

Buddha in the Kitchen

The Buddha's favourite snack is cheese on toast. Cheese, chutney, butter, bread – mmm! Sometimes, however, he finds he has no chutney. Sometimes no butter. Sometimes no bread. Sometimes no cheese. Take away all the ingredients, and what's left? – Oh, please, says the Buddha; that's just ridiculous!

Buddha on Hold

The Buddha has been waiting on a helpline for some time to make a complaint about a failed delivery. He is as reasonable as the next person, but this level of service is quite unacceptable, and he is beginning to become seriously annoyed. – Hang on a moment, the Buddha thinks, I recognise this: the frustration, the anger, the need, so familiar. And to be met with equanimity. He touches the ground with one hand, and hangs up with the other.

Printed in Poland
by Amazon Fulfillment
Poland Sp. z o.o., Wrocław